The Wealth Builder's Handbook: Strategies For Financial Success.

Christopher C. Kincaid

Copyright

All rights reserved. No part of this publication may be reproduced, distributed, or transmitted in any form or by any means, including photocopying, recording, or other electronic or mechanical methods, without the prior written permission of the publisher, except in the case of brief quotations embodied in critical reviews and certain other noncommercial uses permitted by copyright law.

Copyright © (Christopher C. Kincaid), (2023).

Table of Contents

[Chapter One](#)

[Chapter Two](#)

[Chapter Three](#)

[Chapter Four](#)

[Chapter Five](#)

CHAPTER ONE

Introduction

Cash is one of the most critical factors in our lives, but a lot of us battle to control it efficiently. Whether or not it's dwelling paycheck to paycheck, drowning in debt, or feeling overwhelmed by using taxes and investments, the challenges of private finance can appear insurmountable. but it oughtn't to be this manner.

In this book, you may discover the secrets to gaining knowledge of your money and reaching economic freedom. Drawing on years of experience in the subject of personal finance, this guide presents a comprehensive overview of the important ideas and strategies you want to recognize to build a stable economic basis.

From developing finances and decreasing debt to investing accurately and planning for retirement, you may discover ways to take control of your budget and build a higher destiny for yourself and your circle of relatives. With clear explanations, actual-world examples, and realistic guidelines, this ebook is the closest useful resource for absolutely everyone trying to gain economic success.

So if you're prepared to take step one towards a brighter economic destiny, permit's get started. Together, we're going to unlock the secrets to financial freedom and position you in the direction of a lifestyle of abundance and prosperity.

Personal finance refers back to the monetary management of a person or family. It involves making choices about how to exceptionally keep, make investments, and spend money, in addition to a way to manipulate debt and guard belongings. right here are some key ideas related to private finance:
Budgeting: Budgeting entails developing a plan for the way to allocate your income and costs over a given period, which includes a month. This may assist you to understand where your money is going and discover areas in which you can cut back or shop greater.

Budgeting is a crucial aspect of personal finance management. It is a process of creating a financial plan that involves setting financial goals, tracking income and expenses, saving for emergencies, and investing for the future. Budgeting helps to ensure that your income is utilized effectively and also helps you to avoid debts and challenges related to unplanned expenses. This article will discuss some of the tips and steps you can take to create an effective budget plan.

1. Evaluate Your Income and Expenses

The first step in creating a budget is to evaluate your income and expenses. You can do this by making a list of all your sources of income and categorizing your expenses into fixed (rent utilities car payments) and variable expenses (groceries entertainment clothing). This will give you a clear idea of where your money is going and how much disposable income you have.

2. Set Financial Goals

After evaluating your income and expenses the next step is to set clear financial goals. Decide how much you want to save, invest or pay off debts. It is essential to be specific when setting financial goals. If you want to save money, determine how much you want to save each month and make sure it is realistic based on your income and expenses.

3. Identify Areas where You Can Cut Back

Once you have identified your financial goals it is time to identify areas where you can reduce your expenses. By doing this you can free up more money to meet your financial goals. Look for things that you can cut back on such as subscriptions that you do not use dining out or entertainment expenses.

4. Create a Budget

With a clear understanding of your income expenses, financial goals, and potential money-saving strategies it is now time to create a budget. A budget is simply a plan that outlines your earning, saving, and spending for a specific period. Use budgeting tools or apps that can help you track your expenses, monitor your savings and adjust your budget accordingly.

5. Stick to Your Budget

Creating a budget is easy but sticking to it requires discipline and commitment. The key to achieving your financial goals is to stay consistent with your budget plan. Review your budget regularly and make adjustments where necessary. Be sure to track your expenses and avoid overspending and make sure your spending aligns with your financial goals.

In conclusion, budgeting is a crucial aspect of personal finance management. By following these tips you can improve your financial situation, achieve your financial goals and avoid debts and other financial challenges. Remember budgeting requires discipline and commitment but the benefits are well worth the effort.

Saving: Saving refers to putting aside a portion of your profits for future dreams or emergencies. This could include saving for retirement, a down price on a house, or a rainy day fund.

Saving is an essential aspect of financial planning. It involves putting aside a portion of your income for future use. Whether you're saving for a specific goal such as a down payment on a house, a vacation, or a rainy day fund, having money set aside can provide peace of mind and financial security.

There are various reasons why saving is important. First, it allows you to prepare for unexpected expenses such as car repairs, medical bills, and home repairs. Without any savings, you may find yourself in a serious financial crisis when these unexpected expenses arise. Having a savings account can also provide a safety net during times of economic uncertainty or job loss.

In addition to emergencies, saving can also help you achieve your long-term financial goals. Whether it's saving for retirement, a child's education, or a dream vacation, putting money away consistently can help you achieve these goals faster. By setting aside a small amount of money each month and earning interest on it your savings can grow over time.

So how do you start a savings plan? The first step is to set a specific goal. It's important to have a clear understanding of what you're saving for and how much you need to save to achieve that goal. Once you've determined your savings goal it's time to come up with a plan to achieve it.

One of the most effective ways of saving is to automate your savings. By setting up a direct deposit from your paycheck to your savings account you can ensure that a portion of your income is saved before you even have the chance to spend it. This method takes advantage of the principle of "out of sight out of mind" and makes it easy to save consistently.

Another great way to save is to cut back on unnecessary expenses. Reducing your spending on things like eating out entertainment and subscriptions can free up money to put toward your savings. It's also helpful to create a budget and track your spending to identify areas where you can cut back.
It's important to choose the right type of savings account to meet your needs. A basic savings account is a great place to start but depending on your goals you may want to consider other options such as a money market account or a certificate of deposit (CD). Be sure to compare interest rates and fees before choosing a savings account.

In conclusion, saving is an important part of financial planning. By setting clear savings goals and developing a plan to achieve them you can ensure that you're prepared for unexpected expenses and can work towards achieving your long-term financial goals. Whether you're new to saving or a seasoned saver it's never too late to start putting money away for your future.

CHAPTER TWO

Investing

Investing involves putting your cash into belongings to generate a return, such as shares, bonds, mutual funds, or actual property. investing lets you develop your wealth over the long term, but it also carries some level of hazard, as the fee of your investments may additionally differ.

Investing is a smart way to grow your wealth. It involves putting your money into assets that have the potential to increase in value over time. Although there are risks involved in investing it is one of the best ways to build wealth and achieve your financial goals. Whether you are just starting or are an experienced investor there are several important factors to consider before investing your money.

Firstly it is important to determine your investment goals. You need to have a clear idea of what you want to achieve with your investments. For instance, do you want to save up for retirement, improve your cash flow or build a long-term investment portfolio? Setting a clear investment goal will help you choose the right investments and make informed decisions.

Secondly, it is important to do your research. Before investing your money you need to know the ins and outs of the market, the available investment options, and the potential risks. You should also consider the historical returns and compare them with other types of investments. It's important to read news and information from reputable sources that provide insights into the market.

Thirdly, diversification is key. One of the biggest challenges of investing is managing risk. One way to manage risk is by diversifying your investments. This involves spreading your money across different asset classes such as stocks, bonds, real estate, and cash. By diversifying your portfolio you'll be better positioned to weather market downturns and protect your investment.

Fourthly choose the right investment vehicle. There are many investment options available in the market each designed to meet different investment objectives. For instance, stocks are ideal for investors seeking long-term growth, bonds are great for generating regular income and mutual funds are ideal for diversification. Knowing your investment goals and risk tolerance will help you choose the right investment vehicle.

Finally, it's important to have a long-term investment strategy. It's essential to establish a plan and follow it while monitoring your investments regularly. Investing is a long-term strategy and it's not meant to bring in quick returns. It's important to remain patient and disciplined as the market changes and to continue to adjust your investment strategy as your goals shift and change.

In conclusion, investing is an excellent way to grow your wealth but it's important to do your research, have a clear investment strategy and maintain discipline. With the right investment strategy, you can become a successful investor and achieve your financial goals over time.

CHAPTER THREE

Debt management: Debt control refers to the method of paying off debts, inclusive of credit score card balances or scholar loans. This might contain growing a compensation plan, consolidating debts, or negotiating with lenders to lower hobby quotes or prices.

Debt management is an important aspect of personal finance that focuses on helping individuals and families get out of debt and stay out of debt. It involves creating a plan to overcome debt negotiating with creditors and adopting an approach to spending and saving that helps prevent future debt.

The first step in debt management is to assess how much debt you have and the interest rates and fees associated with each debt. Once you have a clear picture of your debt you can begin to create a plan to pay it off. This plan should prioritize debts with the highest interest rates and fees while also ensuring that you make at least minimum payments on all debts to avoid late fees and potential damage to your credit score.

Negotiating with creditors is also an important part of debt management. Depending on your financial situation and the type of debt you have you may be able to negotiate lower interest rates fees or a payment plan that fits your budget. Being proactive and communicating with creditors can help prevent collections and legal action that could result in additional fees and damage to your credit score.

In addition to paying off debt debt management also involves adopting a lifestyle that helps prevent future debt. This means creating a budget tracking expenses and being mindful of your spending habits. Saving money and building an emergency fund can also help prevent future debt by providing a cushion for unexpected expenses.

Seeking professional help from a debt management or credit counseling agency can also be a valuable option for those struggling with debt. These agencies can provide personalized advice and support for creating a debt repayment plan and improving financial habits.

Overall debt management is an important aspect of personal finance that helps individuals and families overcome debt and stay financially stable. It involves creating a plan to pay off debt, negotiating with creditors, and adopting a responsible approach to spending and saving. By taking these steps and seeking professional help when needed anyone can achieve financial freedom and a debt-free future.

CHAPTER FOUR

Asset protection: Asset protection refers to the stairs you can take to defend your assets, which includes insurance, property planning, and setting up criminal protections.

Asset protection is a strategy used to protect assets from potential legal creditors or other risks. Individual families and businesses use this approach to secure their wealth and minimize the risk of financial loss.

Asset protection is the process of organizing your assets and affairs in such a way that they are legally protected from any form of claims or other types of liability. Asset protection methods vary and range from the establishment of legal entities to the use of insurance policies, trusts, and different types of accounts.

One of the most popular methods of asset protection is the creation of a trust. A trust is a legal agreement where the grantor transfers assets to the trustee who then manages and distributes the assets to the beneficiaries according to the terms of the trust document. Trusts offer many advantages including tax savings and protection from creditors.

Limited liability companies (LLCs) are another popular asset protection tool used by many businesses. An LLC can help shield personal assets from business liabilities such as lawsuits or bankruptcy.

Another way to protect assets is through insurance policies such as life insurance home insurance and liability insurance. Insurance policies provide valuable protection for individuals and families ensuring that they are financially protected against risks such as natural disasters, accidents, or liability claims.

Asset protection planning should always be done with a qualified professional such as an estate planning attorney to ensure legal compliance and proper implementation of the chosen strategies. A professional advisor can provide the necessary guidance to maximize asset protection and minimize risks.

In conclusion, protecting your assets is essential to safeguard your wealth and minimize potential liabilities. Different asset protection strategies can help you achieve this goal ranging from the creation of trusts and LLCs to the use of insurance policies. By working with a professional advisor you can develop an effective asset protection plan that meets your specific needs and goals.

setting monetary goals: one of the first steps in dealing with your private finances is to discover your financial desires. This could encompass quick-term dreams, which include paying off credit score card debt or saving for a down price on a house, in addition to long-time period dreams, such as saving for retirement or sending your youngsters to college. Setting clean monetary desires lets you create a plan for how to allocate your profits and charges.

Setting monetary goals is a crucial step toward achieving financial independence and stability. Whether you are saving for a down payment on a home, building an emergency fund, or working towards retirement, having defined monetary goals can help you prioritize your spending and establish a plan to achieve your objectives.

Here are some tips on how to set monetary goals:

1. Determine your current financial situation: Before setting monetary goals it is essential to understand where you stand financially. Assess your income, expenses, debt, and assets to determine your net worth. Knowing your current financial situation will help you develop realistic and achievable monetary goals.

2. Identify your priorities: Consider what is most important to you and the timeframe in which you want to accomplish your goals. Do you want to save for your child's education, pay off debt or take a dream vacation? Once you understand your priorities you can prioritize your goals and allocate your resources accordingly.

3. Set realistic goals: Setting realistic and achievable goals is crucial to staying motivated and committed to your monetary plan. Be specific and measurable when setting your goals. For example, if you want to save for a

down payment on a home, determine the amount you need and the timeframe in which you want to save.

4. Establish a timeline: Creating a timeline for each goal can help you stay on track and motivated. Divide your goal into smaller manageable steps to make it more achievable. For a long-term goal, you can set goals for each year or quarter to ensure you are making progress.

5. Review and adjust your goals regularly: Your monetary goals might change as your circumstances change. Regularly review your goals and adjust them to ensure they remain relevant and achievable.

In conclusion, setting monetary goals is a critical step toward achieving financial stability and independence. It is essential to assess your current situation, identify your priorities, set realistic goals, establish a timeline for each goal, and review and adjust your goals regularly. Taking these steps can help you prioritize your spending and make progress toward achieving your dreams.

Developing a price range: A price range is a plan for a way you'll allocate your income and expenses over a given time frame, which includes a month. There are many one-of-a-kind procedures to budgeting, however, a commonplace method is to music your spending and evaluate it for your profits. This will help you become aware of regions in which you are spending greater than you can manage to pay for, and make changes to your spending conduct.

Developing a price range can be a crucial exercise for individuals and businesses alike. A price range is simply a range of prices that you can charge for your products or services. It is a critical component of your pricing strategy as it helps you determine the most suitable pricing for your target market. If you are unsure how to develop a price range here are several useful tips to get started.

1. Know Your Costs

Before setting any price range you need to know your costs. This includes variable costs such as raw materials manufacturing expenses and labor and fixed costs such as overhead expenses rent and insurance. Knowing your costs will help you determine the minimum price you need to charge to cover your expenses and make a profit. This is important because setting a price range below your costs could lead to financial losses.

2. Identify Your Target Customers

Your pricing strategy should match the needs and preferences of your target customers. Therefore it's vital to understand who your target customers are and what they value the most. Conduct market research to find out their demographic preferences and purchasing behavior. This information will help you decide the most appropriate price range for your products or services.

3. Study Your Competitors

Analyzing your competitors' pricing strategies can help you decide where to position your price range. Check their prices, product quality, and unique selling points. Identify if their products or services are similar or different from yours. This knowledge will help you determine how to differentiate your offerings and make your price range competitive.

4. Consider Market Trends

Studying market trends can help you make informed decisions about your price range. For instance, if demand for your product is high you might be able to charge higher prices. On the other hand, if the market is saturated with similar products or services you might need to set a lower price to compete effectively.

5. Test Your Price Range

After developing your price range, test it with potential customers. Conduct surveys or use focus groups to gather feedback on your pricing strategy. This feedback can help you refine your price range and make it more appealing to customers.

In conclusion, developing a price range can help you price your products or services effectively. By knowing your costs, identifying your target customers, studying your competitors, considering market trends, and testing your price range you can make informed decisions that help your business grow and succeed.

Saving and making an investment: Saving refers to placing apart a portion of your income for future goals or emergencies. This might encompass saving for retirement, a down payment on a house, or a wet day fund. Investing includes putting your cash into assets to produce a return, inclusive of stocks, bonds, mutual price range, or actual property. Investing permits you to develop your wealth over a long time, but it also includes some degree of risk, as the fee of your investments might also vary.

handling debt: Debt control entails paying off money owed, inclusive of credit score card balances or scholar loans. This might contain developing a reimbursement plan, consolidating money owed, or negotiating with lenders to decrease hobby charges or costs. It is crucial to be proactive in coping with debt, as excessive ranges of debt may have a poor impact in your credit score and typical economic fitness.

Protecting belongings: Asset protection refers to the steps you can take to shield your assets, which include insurance, property-making plans, and setting up prison protections. This could encompass buying insurance to protect in opposition to surprising activities, inclusive of a vehicle accident or herbal catastrophe, or creating a will to make certain that your property is allotted in keeping with your wishes when you pass away.

Blessings:
Budgeting can be a beneficial device for dealing with your non-public budget and achieving your financial goals. here are some blessings of budgeting:

allows you to apprehend in which your money is going: A price range permits you to song your spending and notice wherein your cash is being allocated. This may help you pick out areas where you are spending more than you can find the money for, and make adjustments to your spending conduct.

allows you to plot your destiny: by allocating your profits and prices in advance, a budget can help you keep for destiny dreams, which include a down price on a house or retirement.

will let you manage debt: by identifying areas wherein you're overspending, a budget assists you to pay off debt more quickly and keep away from taking up new debt.
Can improve your universal economic fitness: through taking care of your spending and saving habits, budgeting lets you construct wealth and enhance your economic well-being.

however, there are also some capability hazards to budgeting:
Calls for time and effort: creating and preserving a budget calls for area and enterprise. it could be time-eating to music your spending and make adjustments to your budget.

Can be restrictive: A price range can restrict your capacity to spend money on non-important objects or activities. This will be irritating if you experience something like you're lacking in reviews or are unable to fulfill surprising expenses.

May be difficult to stick to: it could be hard to stick to finances, in particular, if you have unexpected charges or changes in your income. It could be tempting to overspend or deviate out of your price range, which can undermine its effectiveness.

Universal budgeting may be a helpful device for dealing with your private price range, but it is crucial to find a balance that works for you.
Saving refers to placing apart a part of your income for future dreams or emergencies.

Right here are a few advantages of saving:
Allows you to plan for destiny: Saving lets you set aside money for long-time period dreams, inclusive of retirement, a down charge on a house, or your children's schooling.
Presents a safety net: Having savings permit you to weather surprising expenses, together with automobile maintenance or medical bills, while not having to go into debt.

Can improve your monetary balance: Having enough financial savings cushion can provide you with peace of mind and enhance your normal economic balance.

Can earn interest: Many savings money owed and different sorts of financial savings motors, together with a certificate of deposit (CDs) and cash marketplace accounts, earn hobby on the cash you deposit. This will help your savings grow over time.

however, there also are a few ability risks to saving:

opportunity fee: by setting aside cash in savings, you will be missing out on the opportunity to earn better returns via investments.

Inflation: The fee of cash tends to say no over time because of inflation, this means that your savings might not be worth as a whole lot in the future as they are today.

restricted entry to a few forms of savings money owed, including CDs, have restrictions on while you can withdraw your cash. This can make it difficult to get the right of entry to your financial savings if you need them unexpectedly.

Common savings is a vital part of private finance, however, it's crucial to discover a balance that works for you. It is useful to set aside a little cash in savings for emergencies and lengthy-term desires, while also investing your cash to doubtlessly earn higher returns.

investing refers back to the act of placing your money into the property to generate a go-back, which includes shares, bonds, mutual price range, or real property. right here are a few blessings of investing:

potential to earn higher returns: by investing your cash, you will be capable of earning a higher return than you'll through other styles of saving or lending, which includes a conventional financial savings account or a certificate of deposit (CD).

opportunity to diversify: investing allows you to unfold your money through a variety of assets, that may help diversify your portfolio and decrease threats.

ability to grow wealth: via investing over the long term, you will be capable of building wealth and attaining your financial goals, together with saving for retirement or shopping for a house.

however, there also are a few capacity disadvantages to investing:
includes chance: The cost of your investments can fluctuate, and there is no guarantee that you may earn a go back for your investment. In truth, it's far possible to lose money via investing.

requires effort and time: investing may be time-consuming because it includes discovering and comparing exclusive funding alternatives and tracking your portfolio.

may be puzzling: the world of investing can be complex and overwhelming, in particular for those who are new to it. It is hard to know where to begin or a way to make knowledgeable investment decisions.

Commonly, investing can be a powerful tool for constructing wealth and reaching your economic goals, however, it's vital to recognize the dangers and do your due diligence before making any funding decisions. It can be beneficial to search for the steerage of a monetary marketing consultant or expert in case you are uncertain approximately how to proceed.

Debt control refers to the process of paying off debts, inclusive of credit score card balances or student loans. right here are a few benefits of debt control:

Can lower interest rates: by consolidating or negotiating with lenders, you'll be capable of securing a decreased hobby fee to your debts, which can save you money ultimately.

Can simplify payments: Debt control techniques, which include consolidation, could make it easier to manage your money owed by streamlining your payments right into a single month-to-month bill.

Can improve credit score: by way of paying off your debts on time and reducing your average debt load, you may be able to improve your credit score, which could have a fine impact on your monetary existence.

however, there are also a few potential disadvantages to debt management:

calls for effort and time: Debt management strategies, which include consolidation and negotiation, can be time-eating and require a vast amount of effort.

may have expenses: some debt control techniques, which include consolidation loans, may additionally have charges related to them.

might not be appropriate for all money owed: Debt management strategies might not be appropriate for all types of money owed, along with secured money owed (e.g. mortgages) or debts that are already at a low hobby rate.

Usually, debt management may be a beneficial device for paying off debts and enhancing your monetary health, but it is important to carefully take into account your options and select a strategy that is appropriate to your wishes. It is useful to be looking for the steering of a monetary guide or expert in case you are uncertain about a way to proceed.

Asset protection refers to the stairs you may take to guard your belongings, together with coverage, estate planning, and putting in legal protections.

Right here are some advantages of asset safety:
Can provide monetary security: by way of protecting your belongings, you can ensure that you have a monetary cushion to fall back on in case of sudden activities, such as a natural disaster or a lawsuit.

will let you achieve your monetary goals: by defending your assets, you could help make sure that you have the sources you need to attain your economic desires, together with saving for retirement or sending your youngsters to college.

Can provide peace of thoughts: Asset safety can provide you with peace of mind by knowing that your property is included and that you have a plan in the vicinity to deal with sudden activities.

But, there also are some capability disadvantages to asset safety:
may contain fees: Asset safety strategies, such as coverage or putting in legal protections, may also have charges associated with them.

may be complicated: Asset protection can be a complicated area of monetary planning, and it can be difficult to know which strategies are most suitable for your wishes.

may not offer complete protection: No asset protection approach is foolproof, and your belongings may nevertheless be at threat in sure situations.

Typically, asset protection is a critical aspect of private finance, however, it is important to carefully recall your alternatives and choose techniques that might be suitable to your needs. It could be beneficial to look for the guidance of a financial advisor or professional if you are uncertain approximately how to continue.

CHAPTER FIVE

Here is a story approximately non-public finance:
Sarah became a 25-year-vintage current university graduate who had just commenced her first full-time activity. She became excited to begin her career, however, she became additionally a little crushed through the responsibility of managing her price range. Up until now, she had depended on her mother and father for financial help, and she wasn't sure where to begin when she got here to manage her cash.

Sarah decided to take control of her price range by way of creating finances. She began by tracking her spending for some weeks to get better expertise on where her money turned into going. She became surprised to discover that she was spending a variety of cash on ingesting out and buying, and little or no on saving or investing.

With this newfound expertise, Sarah made a plan to scale back on her non-critical spending and put greater of her income into financial savings. She also began placing apart money for long-term goals, inclusive of saving for a down charge on a house and constructing an emergency fund.
Sarah additionally took steps to reduce her debt. She consolidated her scholar loans and worked along with her lenders to lower her hobby prices. She also made a plan to pay off her credit card balances as speedy as viable.
Over the years, Sarah's cautious budgeting and debt management paid off. She becomes able to pay off her money owed, build up her financial savings, and begin investing in destiny. She felt a lot greater in control of her price range and became on course to gain her long-time period economic dreams.
different topics relating to non-public finance

Right here are some extra topics which might be associated with personal finance:
credit: credit refers to the potential to borrow money or get entry to other economic assets, consisting of credit playing cards or loans. Building and retaining an awesome credit rating is crucial for getting access to credit scores at favorable terms and costs, and for attaining your monetary goals.
credit rankings: A credit score rating is a numerical illustration of your creditworthiness, based totally on facts in your credit file. Credit rankings are utilized by lenders, landlords, and others to assess your credit risk and decide your capability to pay again money owed.

credit score reviews: A credit score file is a report of your credit score records, inclusive of statistics about your borrowing and compensation pastime. Credit reviews are used to generate credit scores and can be vital for having access to credit and other financial opportunities.

Retirement-making plans: Retirement-making plans entail preparing for your economic needs during retirement, along with saving for retirement and developing a plan for the way to generate profits during retirement.
estate making plans: property making plans involve making ready for the switch of your assets after you bypass away, including through the introduction of a will or accept as true. property planning can assist make certain that your belongings are distributed according to your desires and might assist reduce taxes and other fees.

Taxes: Taxes are expenses that are levied by using governments on individuals and corporations to fund public services and applications. expertise and dealing with your tax duties are vital components of private finance.
decision making refers back to the method of choice amongst alternatives. It is a fundamental part of personal finance, as financial choices will have extensive results on your financial well-being. right here are some key issues whilst making monetary choices:

desires: earlier than creating a monetary decision, it's essential to not forget your desires and how the selection will impact your ability to attain them.
As an example, if your purpose is to save for retirement, you may prioritize making an investment by overspending on non-important objects.
alternate-offs: monetary decisions frequently contain exchange-offs, meaning that you have to weigh the pros and cons of different alternatives. For example, you would possibly have to decide between saving cash and spending cash on something that brings you instantaneous delight.

hazard: financial selections can involve dangers, which include the chance of losing money or missing out on potential possibilities. It's crucial to take into account the level of hazard you are comfortable with and how it would affect your economic well-being.

statistics: appropriate decision-making often involves collecting and reading statistics approximately the options available to you. This could consist of searching financial statements, comparing fees, or searching for the advice of a monetary expert.
emotions: emotions can play a function in monetary selection-making, and it's vital to be privy to how your feelings would possibly affect your judgment. For instance, you might feel pressured to shop for something because of a fear of missing out, otherwise, you are probably overly optimistic about a funding opportunity.

through thinking about those factors, you may make extra knowledgeable financial choices that are aligned with your dreams and danger tolerance. It's also crucial to be flexible and open to revising your selections as your situations or priorities trade.

Here are a few extra issues when it comes to economic choice-making:
Time horizon: The time horizon of a financial selection refers to the length of time over which it will have an impact. long-time period economic decisions, together with saving for retirement or buying a residence, tend to have an extended time horizon and might require an extraordinary method than short-time period choices, such as deciding what to eat for dinner tonight.

opportunity price: possibility value refers to the potential benefits that you give up through choosing one alternative over another. For instance, if you decide to shop for cash by no longer going out to eat, the possible price is probably the enjoyment you will be getting from the eating place.

The margin of protection: The margin of protection is the distinction between the fee of funding and the fee you pay for it. a larger margin of protection can offer a buffer towards capability losses and decrease threat.

Sunk cost fallacy: The sunk fee fallacy refers back to the tendency to preserve investing in something because of the money or time already invested, even if it is not a terrific selection. It is vital to take into account the destiny capability of funding, rather than simply the money or assets already invested.

By considering those and different elements, you can make more informed and strategic monetary choices that can be aligned with your dreams and threat tolerance. It is also important to be open to learning and revising your selections as you benefit from new data or your trade situations.

Right here are some measures you could take to improve your financial decision-making:

Set dreams: surely described goals can help manual your economic decisions and make certain that you are working closer to what is important to you.

accumulate records: before creating a financial decision, it could be beneficial to acquire as much data as possible approximately the alternatives to be had to you. This might include looking at monetary statements, evaluating expenses, or looking for the advice of an economic expert.

take into account the trade-offs: economic selections frequently contain alternate-offs, so it's crucial to weigh the pros and cons of different alternatives.

Be aware of your feelings: feelings can affect economic choice-making, so it is important to be aware of how your emotions may affect your judgment.
seek recommendation: if you are unsure about a financial choice, it could be useful to be looking for the advice of a monetary expert or a trusted pal or member of the family.

by following those steps, you may enhance your financial selection-making and make alternatives that can be aligned with your desires and threat tolerance. It is also essential to be bendy and open to revising your selections as you gain new statistics or your circumstances alternate.
Finance is the study of how human beings, organizations, and corporations manipulate and allocate economic assets over time. It includes the evaluation of financial facts, the development of economic techniques, and the implementation of economic plans.

Private finance is the utility of finance standards to the economic control of a character or family. It entails making selections about how to store, invest, and spend money to obtain economic goals, consisting of shopping for a residence, saving for retirement, or paying off debt.

enterprise finance is the application of finance standards to the monetary management of a business. It involves making choices about the way to raise and allocate economic assets to fund operations, put money into growth, and attain financial dreams.

Corporate finance is a subfield of enterprise finance that specializes in the economic decisions of big, publicly-traded agencies. It entails studying economic information, growing financial techniques, and raising and allocating financial assets to fund operations and boom.

Public finance is the examination of ways governments improve and allocate monetary resources. It involves the evaluation of government budgets, the development of monetary coverage, and the control of presidential debt.

Finance is a vast and complex field, and it touches on many elements of personal, commercial enterprise, and public life. It's miles an important region of study for all and sundry seeking to understand and manipulate financial resources effectively.

www.ingramcontent.com/pod-product-compliance
Lightning Source LLC
Chambersburg PA
CBHW030046230526
45472CB00005B/1703